Set it on Fire

STUDY GUIDE

Cover design by Sara Young
Cover photo by: Andrew van Tilborgh

ISBN: 978-1-959095-99-6   1 2 3 4 5 6 7 8 9 10

Printed in the United States of America

THE ART OF
INNOVATION

Set it on Fire

NATALIE M. BORN

STUDY GUIDE

AVAIL

CONTENTS

NATALIE M. BORN

THE ART OF
INNOVATION

Set it on Fire

STRONG FOUNDATIONS ALWAYS ACCELERATE INNOVATION

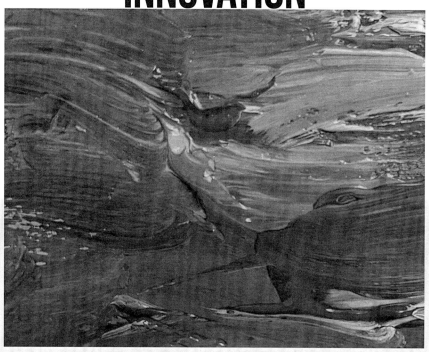

"Anything you build should be on the foundation of your vision, mission, values, and goals."

READING
TIME

As you read
Chapter 1:
"Strong
Foundations
Always
Accelerate
Innovation" in
Set It on Fire,
reflect on the
questions.

REFLECT AND TAKE ACTION:

What four things comprise the foundation of your organization? How would you rate your organization's foundation? What can you do to improve it and make it sturdier?

1._____

_____

2._____

_____

3._____

_____

4._____

_____

_____

_____

_____

_____

What is your organization's vision? Is your vision well-written, clear, memorable, and concise? If not, which of these attributes is missing?

_____

_____

_____

_____

_____

_____

_____

What is your organization's mission? Does your mission push your team toward a common goal, empower your team to act, and effectively explain what you do and for whom you do it?

_____

_____

_____

_____

_____

What are your organizational values? Have these changed over the years? How do you live these values out?

_____

_____

_____

_____

_____

What are your current goals for your company? How do you measure improvement? What needs to change in order for you to grow?

_____

_____

_____

_____

_____

Is your decision framework aligned with your vision, mission, company values, and goals? Explain.

_____

_____

_____

Of the roles of a leader discussed, which do you feel you do well, and which do you need to work on? Which team roles discussed does your team do well, and which do they need to work on?

_____

_____

_____

_____

_____

_____

What needs to change about your organization to bring its vision, mission, values, and goals into alignment? Take time to devise some action steps you can take to move in the right direction.

_____

_____

_____

_____

_____

_____

_____

"GET OUT OF MY SANDBOX!" WHY TEAMING IS A LINCHPIN FOR INNOVATION

"Does your culture reward the team working together, or does it reward an every-man-for-himself mentality?"

As you read Chapter 2: "Get Out of My Sandbox!" Why Teaming is a Linchpin for Innovation" in *Set It on Fire*, reflect on the questions.

REFLECT AND TAKE ACTION:

What does it mean to take ideas internal? Why might this be a good idea?

_____

_____

_____

_____

_____

_____

_____

_____

_____

_____

What can you do to promote collaboration within your organization? Would you say your current culture rewards collaboration? Why or why not?

_____

_____

_____

_____

_____

_____

_____

_____

_____

_____

_____

What is an organizational silo? Why is this not an optimal environment for innovation to occur?

_____

_____

_____

_____

_____

_____

What does it mean to take ideas external? How does this differ from taking ideas internally, and why might a leader choose this option?

_____

_____

_____

_____

_____

_____

Which of the five attributes that drive success (dependability, structure and clarity, meaning of work, impact of work, psychological safety) do you need to work on providing for your team? How can you do this practically?

_____

_____

_____

_____

_____

_____

_____

DOES YOUR CULTURE KILL OR CULTIVATE INNOVATION?

"Strong organizations work in a high-trust environment, creating team health and driving people toward the outcomes they want to hit as a company."

As you read
Chapter 3:
"Does Your
Culture Kill
or Cultivate
Innovation?"
in *Set It on Fire*,
reflect on the
questions.

REFLECT AND TAKE ACTION:

Does your organization struggle with alignment? If so, in what areas?

_____

_____

_____

_____

_____

_____

_____

_____

_____

_____

What are your strategic targets? How often do you talk about them with your team? How do you measure them? How do you celebrate them?

_____

_____

_____

_____

_____

_____

_____

_____

_____

_____

Do you feel your team is healthy? How would you define a team's health?

_____

_____

_____

_____

_____

Do you use empathy when formulating a new product or service? How do you think doing this may benefit your organization?

_____

_____

_____

_____

_____

_____

Of the four ways to listen (coffee conversations, listening sessions, surveys, observation) which do you do best? Which could your organization benefit from implementing?

_____

_____

_____

_____

_____

_____

How can you learn more about your ideal customers and clients?

_____

_____

_____

_____

_____

How would you define your leadership persona? Are you content with this persona? What, if anything, would you like to change?

_____

_____

_____

_____

_____

What practical organizational steps can you take to implement some of the methodology discussed in this chapter?

_____

_____

_____

_____

_____

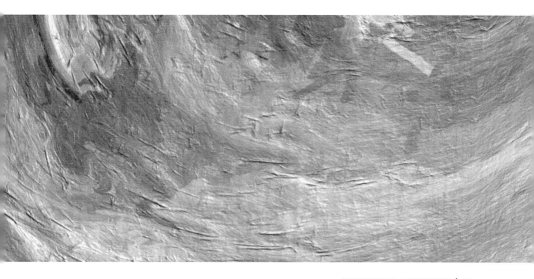

GET OUT THERE AND SEE THE WORLD—THE ULTIMATE SOCIALIZATION FRAMEWORK

"Innovation is no longer about brilliant individuals; it's about brilliant teams."

READING TIME

As you read Chapter 4: "Get Out There and See the World—The Ultimate Socialization Framework" in *Set It on Fire*, reflect on the questions.

REFLECT AND TAKE ACTION:

Would you consider your current team a dream team? Why or why not?

_____

_____

_____

_____

_____

_____

_____

_____

_____

_____

Why do you think perfectionism can be so harmful to innovation?

_____

_____

_____

_____

_____

_____

_____

_____

_____

_____

_____

What can you do to promote your team to release ideas quickly instead of holding onto them until the opportunity is missed?

_____

_____

_____

_____

_____

_____

_____

How does feedback benefit innovation? What sources of consumer feedback does your organization currently have?

_____

_____

_____

_____

_____

_____

How does one "batch" feedback? Of the four types discussed (out of scope, small changes, large changes, product backlog) which do you feel is the most common for consumers to give feedback on?

_____

_____

_____

_____

_____

_____

What is one idea your team has been pitching for a while now that has never come to fruition? What steps can you take today to take this idea from the drawing board to the field?

_____

_____

_____

_____

_____

_____

_____

IT'S TIME TO GROW UP

"So, how mature is your organization when it comes to these three areas: pace, processes, and empowerment? These areas help or hurt an organization's ability to innovate."

READING TIME

As you read Chapter 5: "It's Time to Grow Up" in *Set It on Fire*, reflect on the questions.

REFLECT AND TAKE ACTION:

Most organizations fail their people in one of three ways: pace, process, and empowerment. Which category do you feel your organization could do better in?

_____

_____

_____

_____

_____

_____

_____

_____

_____

_____

What is the pace of an organization? What is the pace of your organization, and are you happy with its pace?

_____

_____

_____

_____

_____

_____

_____

_____

_____

_____

What is the danger of a lack of processes for an organization? Does your organization have apt processes?

_____

_____

_____

_____

_____

_____

_____

How does your organization empower its people? How do you empower those you lead?

_____

_____

_____

_____

_____

_____

_____

Of the five CMMI organizational maturity levels discussed in this chapter, what level is your organization at? What practical steps would take it to the next level?

_____

_____

_____

_____

_____

_____

_____

_____

What principles about leading change stand out to you from this chapter? Are there any you did not know or were not aware of?

_____

_____

_____

_____

_____

_____

_____

_____

How can you better lead your organization into and through change?

_____

_____

_____

_____

_____

_____

_____

THE PRODUCT DEVELOPMENT FRAMEWORK

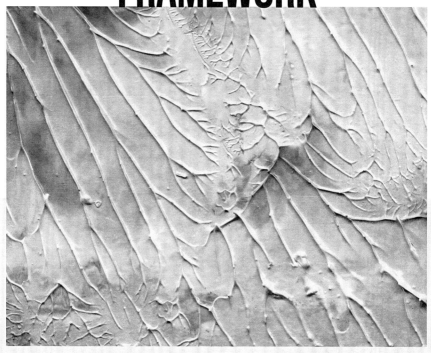

"Innovation can be both 'bottom-up' and 'top-down.'"

As you read
Chapter 6:
"The Product
Development
Framework" in
Set It on Fire,
reflect on the
questions.

REFLECT AND TAKE ACTION:

In what ways does your organization surface new ideas?

_____

_____

_____

_____

_____

_____

Has your organization ever hosted a business plan competition? What do you think are the pros and cons of something like this for your organization?

_____

_____

_____

_____

_____

_____

_____

What is a Hackathon? Has your organization ever had a hackathon? Why or why not?

_____

_____

_____

_____

_____

_____

What is customer incubation? How might this strategy give you new and effective innovation, product, and service ideas?

_____

_____

_____

_____

_____

_____

_____

Does your origination have a product development framework like the one in this chapter? What steps are you missing? What steps do you have that aren't in the framework provided?

_____

_____

_____

_____

_____

_____

_____

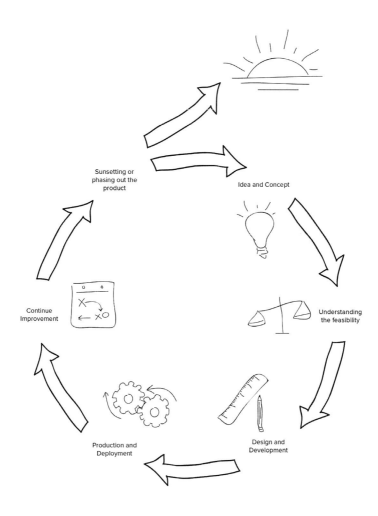

Idea and Concept

Understanding the feasibility

Design and Development

Production and Deployment

Continue Improvement

Sunsetting or phasing out the product

How will you measure your success? Take time to build a scorecard that draws from the measurements and examples provided near the end of the chapter.

_____

_____

_____

_____

_____

_____

_____

FAILURE: INNOVATION'S TRAINING GROUND

"... fail fast, fail cheap, and rise smarter."

READING TIME

As you read Chapter 7: "Failure: Innovation's Training Ground" in *Set It on Fire*, reflect on the questions.

REFLECT AND TAKE ACTION:

Do you fear failure when it comes to innovation? Why or why not?

_____

_____

_____

_____

_____

_____

_____

_____

_____

_____

_____

Describe a time your organization attempted innovation and failed. What went wrong? What did you learn from this situation?

_____

_____

_____

_____

_____

_____

_____

_____

_____

_____

_____

_____

Do you think your organization's culture is currently accepting of failure and encouraging when someone fails? What can you do to facilitate this?

_____

_____

_____

_____

_____

_____

_____

Of the popular failures discussed, which jumps out to you? What stands out to you from this story, and what can you learn from their failure?

_____

_____

_____

_____

_____

_____

_____

In your own words, how would you define the difference between "failures" and "mistakes"?

_____

_____

_____

_____

_____

_____

_____

Why do you think someone's mindset surrounding failure is so important?

_____

_____

_____

_____

_____

_____

When hiring, do you look for someone who has failed before and is comfortable with failure? Why or why not?

_____

_____

_____

_____

_____

_____

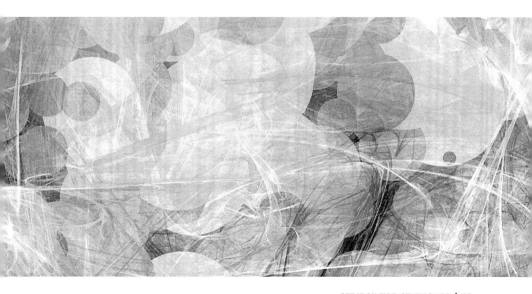

HUMAN-CENTERED DESIGN AND VISUAL AGREEMENT

"If meeting culture is a reflection of company culture, we have some work to do in organizations if we want to run fun and effective meetings."

READING TIME

As you read Chapter 8: "Human-Centered Design and Visual Agreement" in *Set It on Fire*, reflect on the questions.

REFLECT AND TAKE ACTION:

Do you assign roles when conducting meetings? If so, what roles do you assign? If not, why?

_____

_____

_____

_____

_____

_____

_____

_____

_____

_____

What visual aspects do you employ during meetings? Do you think you can work more visually? If so, what?

_____

_____

_____

_____

_____

_____

_____

_____

_____

_____

How do you follow up and follow through with the decisions you make within meetings? How often do decisions fizzle out and never come to fruition?

_____

_____

_____

_____

_____

_____

_____

What is your organization's meeting culture? Does it mirror your organization's culture as a whole?

_____

_____

_____

_____

_____

_____

_____

How do you go about preparing for a meeting? What could you do better in this stage?

_____

_____

_____

_____

_____

_____

_____

When you are hosting the meeting, do you create goals? Which of the bullet points listed in this chapter do you need to better focus on?

_____

_____

_____

_____

_____

_____

_____

_____

How can you better follow up after conducting meetings?

_____

_____

_____

_____

_____

_____

_____

Which stage of the "Open, Explore, Close" process does your organization most struggle with? Why do you think this is?

_____

_____

_____

_____

_____

_____

_____

_____

INNOVATION FUNDING AND FRAMEWORK

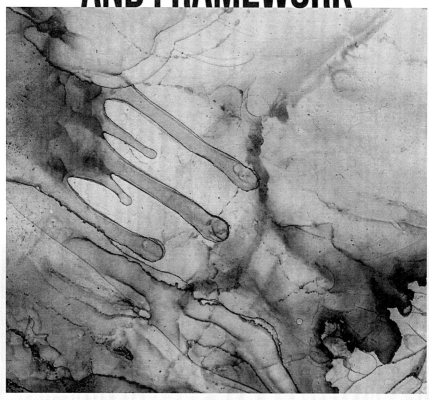

"Oftentimes, boundaries—not endless pools of money—are what help us innovate."

READING TIME

As you read Chapter 9: "Innovation Funding and Framework" in *Set It on Fire*, reflect on the questions.

REFLECT AND TAKE ACTION:

What is freedom in a framework? What could it look like for your organization?

_____

_____

_____

_____

_____

_____

_____

_____

_____

_____

When has your organization made a transformative innovation? What was the result?

_____

_____

_____

_____

_____

_____

_____

_____

_____

_____

_____

_____

How often does your organization have a breakthrough innovation? When and what was your last breakthrough innovation?

_____

_____

_____

_____

_____

_____

_____

Has your organization ever had a disruptive innovation? What was it?

_____

_____

_____

_____

_____

_____

What is your organization's current stance on funding innovation? How could this improve?

_____

_____

_____

_____

_____

_____

_____

Do you find your organization favoring one type of innovation over the other two? Which? Why do you think this is?

_____

_____

_____

_____

_____

_____

_____

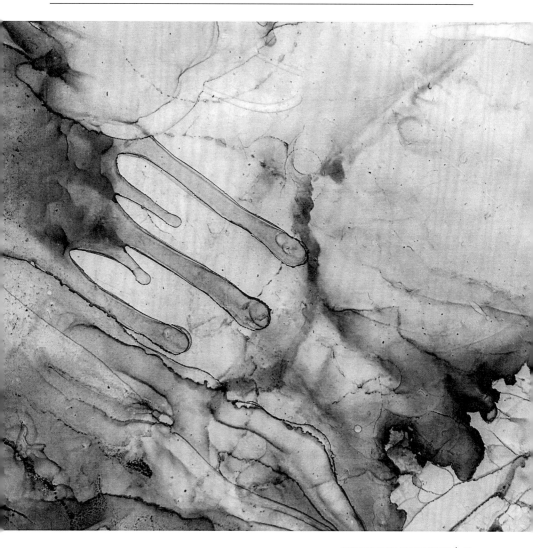

POSITION YOUR PRODUCT AND LAUNCH LIKE A PRO

"Don't just get out of the box. Break the box, and set it on fire."

READING TIME

As you read Chapter 10: "Position Your Product and Launch Like a Pro" in *Set It on Fire*, reflect on the questions.

REFLECT AND TAKE ACTION:

When it comes to launching a product, what is on your checklist? What else do you think you need to add?

_____

_____

_____

_____

_____

_____

_____

_____

_____

_____

Where do you currently go for testimonials? How else can you collect testimonials when you launch a new product or service?

_____

_____

_____

_____

_____

_____

_____

_____

_____

_____

_____

Do you currently utilize a marketing cadence when promoting your products? Why or why not? If not, do you think this could bring more success?

_____

_____

_____

_____

_____

_____

When is the last time your organization conducted a thought leadership roundtable? How do you think this may benefit your organization and its flow of ideas?

_____

_____

_____

_____

_____

_____

What can you begin to build now as you see your product launch on the horizon?

_____

_____

_____

_____

_____

_____

How do you want your product to be received by the market?

_____

_____

_____

_____

_____

_____

What will you do to promote your product once it officially launches?

_____

_____

_____

_____

_____

_____